DISCERNMENT

Seasons of Delusion, Devotion, and Deliverance

By Dr. Corey Castillo

What must we see, within ourselves and within others, in order to navigate life so as to experience it as best we can? In other words, what must we be able to discern so that we may *live well*? This book is a short collection of interpretations – or thoughts – that seek to answer such a question. Each interpretation was directly influenced by the observations and reflections one man experienced during one year of his life, as he paused to observe himself, and others, in life's seasons of *Delusion, Devotion, and Deliverance*.

CONTENTS

INTRODUCTION

Dr. Corey Castillo is quite possibly the least likely to be considered "poetic" by those who know him. Professionally, he is a business strategist and an executive leader. However, throughout various conversations, over the span of one year, he found himself saying "more with less" more and more, as it pertained to exploring and framing fundamental interpretations [of life]. This naturally began to feel rather *poetic*. While most interpretations were explored for purposes of decision making (within the context of the respective moments in which they were observed), nearly all held a common theme around discernment – or seeking to *see* life more clearly – in an effort to *live well*.

While recognizing that our interpretations [of life] don't always occur in full thought, but sometimes in short insightful gems or axioms, Corey recorded a year's worth of interpretations in a rather poetic style— as personal quotes and as they occurred to him. This, not for the sake of "sounding poetic" in it of itself, but rather to capture their meaning in a fashion that other, more explanatory, styles of writing could not.

In this effort, Corey recorded at least one interpretation each week, for one year, based upon what he saw and his reflections thereof— doing so without filter or worry of critics (whether actual or imagined). As a result, he wrote *Discernment: Seasons of Delusion, Devotion, and Deliverance.*

…this collection is dedicated to my wife, Christine.

AUTHOR'S NOTE

"This collection of interpretations – or thoughts, key notes, personal quotes, short poems, statements, whatever one may call them – was a one-year project dedicated to recording currently held perspectives. It was a year dedicated to reflecting on self, others, our nature, and the roles we play while interacting with life. It was a project focused on exploring one question: What must we be able to discern so that we may *live well?*

While these personal quotes are, by no means, complete, they are a collection of interpretations gathered during a one-year snapshot of my life. Nothing more. I wrote them for my own expression and reflection. I published them to share with others who may find interest as they please.

Throughout this year, I saw others, and depictions of myself, living within three distinct mindsets, by which I refer to as [seasons of] *Delusion, Devotion,* and *Deliverance*, and which correspond to three terrains, by which I refer to as *The Desert, The Forest,* and *The Mountains.* While living within these mindsets, I noticed we assume different roles as we interact with life, ourselves, and one another.

This short collection sheds light on the roles I saw…"

-Corey

THE DESERT: *Seasons of Delusion*

The desert is a place of frustration and anger, influenced by a mindset that may be described as vain and juvenile. In the desert, we tend to interpret the world from a perspective that is limited by our own feelings and with little regard for matters beyond ourselves. It symbolizes the seasons of life in which we tend to reject what "is" (reality) while living with a sense of delusion.

These are the roles I saw others, and depictions of myself, playing during the times in which we've chosen to live in delusion...

The Empty

Unspoken virtuousness bears humility.
It is full in its own deeds.

Spoken virtuousness bears narcissism.
It is empty in its own praise.

*...For virtue is not a public posture of nobility
entertained by cheap praise. It is a private discipline
anchored by its own conviction.*

The Damned

Self-justification of wrongdoing is simply
recognition of guilt without admission.

It is deception disguised as reason, for acts of right
doing require no self-justification.

It is the first page written in a story of destruction.

It is the language of the damned.

The Outraged

Far too many have made blame a virtue and outrage to an instinct. In this, the common scapegoat has become a sacred cow.

It is destined to crumble by its own weight.

...For those who pursue power through blame do not find power at all, but rather steal an illusion of power from greater contenders with heavier burdens. They will always fall.

The Inferior

The man who postures a moral superiority seen before others carries a dangerous inferiority unseen before himself.

The Inferior II

The man who seeks to be equal among all,
ignores greatness both in himself and in others.

He is not humble. For to be humble, he must honor
the greatness of others before, and unequal to, himself.

He is not free. For to be free, he must honor
the pursuit of greatness beyond, and unequal to, others.

He is inferior in his resentment
of himself and others.

The Naïve

Falsehoods are falsehoods,
even when dressed as idealism.

Naivety is naivety,
even when dressed as purity.

The Naïve II

The moment we choose to fall victim to the idea that we are sewn from a cloth any different from those, who we decry as delusional, is the moment we, ourselves, become susceptible to that same delusion.

The Indifferent

This world has no shortage of those who denounce the claims of others yet hold no claims of their own…

…who decry the wrongness of others yet draw no lines on rightness of their own.

It is better to stand for something and carry the weight of persecution, than to stand for anything and carry nothing at all.

The indifferent choose not to know such an honorable burden.

The Hateful

That, which we allow ourselves to hate,
draws us to become a lesser version of itself.

The Neutral

We are never truly neutral.

To pretend so is to deny our respect for self. To act so is to deny our respect for another.

The Foolish

The foolish sacrifice influence
for attention.

The wise sacrifice attention
for influence.

The Prideful

Pride and guilt live in the same house
but seldom recognize one another.

The Wicked

Pride knows no boundaries between itself
and the rebellion it becomes.

Rebellion knows no boundaries between itself
and the wickedness it becomes.

The Entitled

Entitlement will drown in a sea of anger,
believing it is owed more.

Humility will sail in a sea of gratitude
knowing it is owed nothing.

The Unhappy

Creating an idol of happiness reflects nothing but a void of happiness.

The Unhappy II

The pursuit of happiness over meaning
kills both happiness and meaning.

The Absurd

To submit to truth
is to know freedom.

To submit to self
is to know absurdity.

The Absurd II

In the eyes of the absurd, life's design, itself, appears absurd.

The Absurd III

Absurdity will always knock on our door. To answer it is to become it.

The Absurd IV

Absurdity cannot see itself,
not even its own shadow.

The Distracted

There are far too many cutting into their own flesh while decrying the world as responsible for their wounds.

The Irrational

To appease the irrational is to feed a demon that knows no limits.

The Disguised

We tend to reveal who we are
with claims of who we are not.

We tend to reveal who we hope to be
with claims of who we are.

The Trapped

History does not repeat itself,
man does.

The Addicted

There is no greater act of foolishness than to escape
death in an idol only to blindly return to the false
promised offered by that same idol.

The Relativist

The relativist claims there are no absolute truths
but I ask, is that an absolute statement?

The relativist claims all is inherently subjective
but I ask, is that an objective standard?

The relativist claims morality may fluctuate
but I ask, what then is a moral dilemma?

The relativist claims a path towards enlightenment
but I ask, where does a path without direction lead?

The Relativist II

Relativism, unhinged, is a thief of accountability and a murderer of glory.

The Relativist III

When any value is placed above truth,
we lose both.

The Deceived

None of us believe that it is us
who dance with the devil,
until it is us standing in our own ruins
and our dear friend, the devil,
is nowhere to be found.

The Vain

The greatest lie man deals himself is the idea that he may *progress* beyond the limitations of his nature.

It is in this lie that man torments himself with attempting to create a heaven, only to find hell.

The Narcissist

The narcissist presents not as a boastful fool
but as an enlightened savior and a noble friend.

Yet, underneath its skin, it is a false idol. It is
compelled by its own image and fed by a hollow
praise.

It is committed to a false justice and determined to
devour anyone who dares shed light on its emptiness.

It hates you…
It hates me…
It hates God…

It hates itself.

*…For narcissism is a cunning spirit, justified by its
own will. While seeing it in another, we must
remember how quickly it may dwell in us.*

The Narcissist II

To desire power
but to reject responsibility
is nothing more
than a contradiction behind
an infatuation with self.

The Chaotic

Chaos is a convenient place to hide.

Chaos is a convenient place to hide
from the burden of accountability.

Chaos is a convenient place to hide
from the accountability of order.

Chaos is a convenient place to hide
from the order of truth.

Chaos is a convenient place to hide
from chaos, itself.

The Chaotic II

A heart in chaos will always demonize truth
while still longing for its rescue

…from the torment it inflicts upon itself.

The Heckler

To heckle is to willingly choose the role of a joker
in a game of kings and queens.

The Irritable

Our irritations by others
are windows into our own inadequacies,
and our longing to conquer them.

The Self-Tormented

Resentment insults responsibility
in the need for comfort.

The Resentful

Beware those who speak not in a will for their own rising but in a will for the fall of others.

For they would rather live in hell, alongside another, than to see anyone taste a piece of heaven that they, themselves, choose not pursue.

The Delusional

Man's greatest enemy is man, himself. For it is in his nature to marvel at his own image, fall by his own works, and marvel again.

This is delusion.

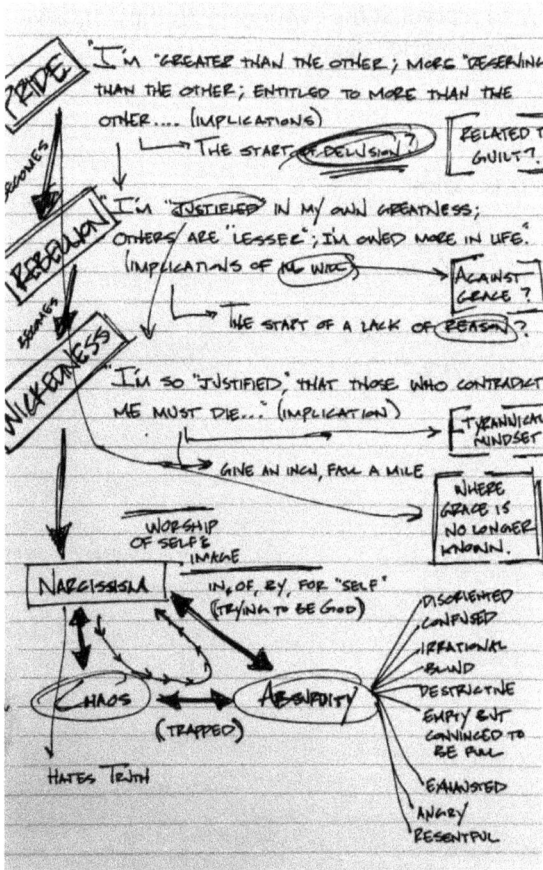

Seasons of Delusion

THE FOREST: *Seasons of Devotion*

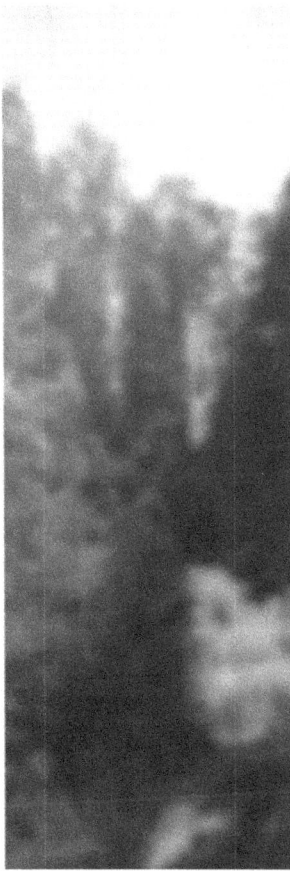

The forest is a place of realization and growth, influenced by a mindset that may be described as strong and enduring. In the forest, we tend to interpret the world from a perspective that reconciles our feelings with respect for matters beyond ourselves. It symbolizes the seasons of life in which we chose to realize what "is" (reality) while living with a sense of devotion.

These are the roles I saw others, and depictions of myself, playing during the times in which we've chosen to live in devotion...

The Grateful

They say life gives us lemons. It wasn't until I stopped trying to force lemonade that I began to cherish life's bitter taste.

The Glorious

There no such thing as glory without suffering. Yet, there is such a thing as suffering without glory.

Remember this in times of suffering.

The Sober

Look at the origin of pain
and see glory.

Look at the owner of pain
and see self.

Look at pain, itself,
and see meaning.

The Light

We are vessels,
full with ideas.

Ideas we do not hold in our hands
but that hold us in theirs.

Understand…

It was an idea, born from darkness,
that ruined temples that once touched the skies.

It will be an idea, born from light,
that will rebuild those temples once again.

The Faithful

It is only in adversity that our convictions
are invited to either become acts in faith
or claims never lived.

The Faithful II

We all have a faith,
even when we don't claim it.

We all have a fundamental value,
even when we don't know it.

We all have a point in which
knowledge rests and belief rises.

We all pursue that which is God,
even when we don't accept it.

The Trusting

Our recognition of truth provides a north star. Our trust in truth keeps that star shining during dark travels.

The Grounded

Our truest nature is revealed
not by our greatest of deeds,
but by our smallest of habits,

…not in the calm of smooth sails,
but in the midst of harsh storms.

The Resolute

You may be cast a villain
but by who's story?

You may be scrutinized
but by who's testament?

You may be condemned
but by who's scorn?

You will see…
slander will always thirst for blood
but from a sacrifice not of its own.

You will know…
slander will always come
but never from greater players.

The Steadfast

Language is the expression of our pursuit of truth. It is our primary vehicle in the formation of self.

To allow others to control our language is to allow others to control self.

To allow others to control self is to allow others to create self in their image.

It is this that reveals how truth may be slowly killed with what begins as the threat of a single word.

The Unwavering

Without a line drawn between honor and dishonor,
we are left to wonder an endless field of *everything*,
with a heart open to receive *anything,* including that
which will ultimately destroy us.

The wise choose to know where this line is drawn.

The unwavering choose to uphold it.

The Disciplined

Motivation is an excitement
infatuated with the idea of tomorrow.

It is fueled by a vision.

Discipline is an ethic
devoted the calling of today.

It is fueled by a belief.

Only one persists when the other fails.

The Champion

The man who chooses the path of the victim may receive sympathy but waives his right to company in glory.

The man who chooses the path of the victor may receive glory but waives his right to company in sympathy.

The man who seeks both may receive no company at all.

The Determined

When the playing field crumbles, the rules of the game become anyone's call.

Those with the clearest vision, and the greatest conviction, will initiate the rules of the new game.

The Gritty

Commentators are seldom contenders,
for they are distracted by the utterances
of their own tongue.

Contenders are seldom commentators,
for they are devoted by the works
of their own hands.

The Absolute

In the relative, we may receive applause.

In the relative, we may receive ridicule.

In the relative, we may never know the difference.

It is better to be truly hated in the absolute
than falsely loved in the relative.

The Willing

Our greatest gift bears the heaviest cost. Pay it
willingly.

The Respectful

Respect is not fueled by recognition *from* another, but by reciprocity *for* another.

The Victorious

The path to victory, in any war, begins with knowing the terrain upon which it is fought, and declaring its name.

This includes the wars we fight within ourselves.

The Committed

Idlers build dependences with lesser idlers,
in a shared numbness.

Champions build alliances with greater champions,
in a shared devotion.

The Committed II

Those who love only treasures
fail in the pursuit for them.

Those who love the pursuit
succeed in earning many treasures.

The Trustful

Place trust in another,
not just with a belief in another's ability,
nor just with a confidence in another's intent,
but with an understanding of another's nature.

For a bird's nature will always be to fly,
as a scorpion's nature will always be to sting.

The Daring

Stories of greatness are written
not by those with a critical eye
but by those with a daring heart.

The Devoted

They say things will get easier...

This is often untrue, they may not,
but it is the uneasy path that bears fruit.

They say the pain will go away...

This is often untrue, it may not,
but it is the painful path that delivers growth.

This path is always a choice.

This is devotion.

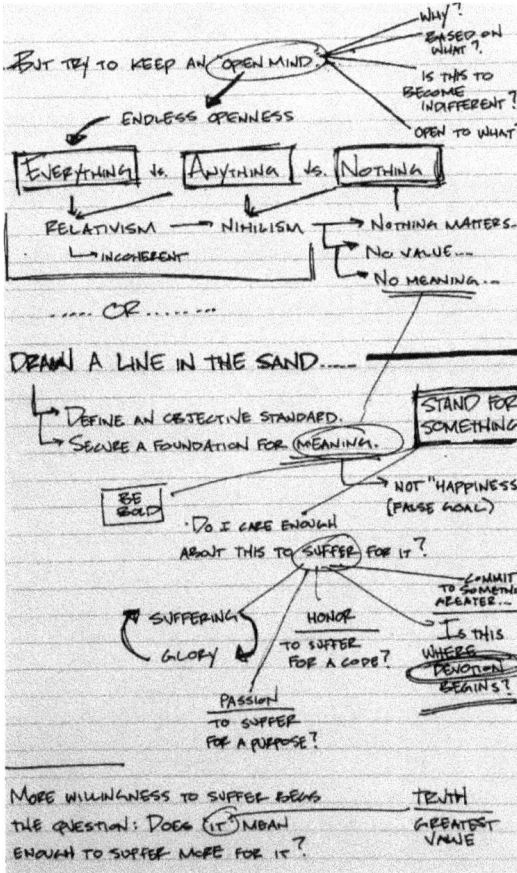

Seasons of Devotion

THE MOUNTAINS: *Seasons of Deliverance*

The mountains are a place of peace and meaning, influenced by a mindset that may be described as matured and graceful. In the mountains, we tend to interpret the world from a perspective that extends far beyond feelings, with a high regard for truth and matters beyond ourselves. It symbolizes the seasons of life in which we chose to embrace what "is" (reality) while living with a sense of deliverance.

These are the roles I saw others, and depictions of myself, playing during the times in which we've chosen to live in deliverance...

The Meaningful

The pursuit of happiness often overlooks a story of meaning. Yet, the pursuit of meaning seldom misses a chapter of happiness.

The Meaningful II

Meaning is never something to be found,
often something to be created,
yet always something to be recognized.

The True

Understand, popular "truth" is untruthful,
and truthful truth is unpopular.

The Clear

Seek not clarity but discernment,
for clarity will come.

The Clear II

…and in that moment, I realized darkness is not a
force, in it of itself, but the mere absence of light.

The Full

The best thing about life is that it's not fair.

The worst thing about life is that it's not fair.

This, itself, is the beauty that is life.

...To search for fairness,
in the many names we may call it,
is to find emptiness in a life that does not exist.

...To live in vulnerability,
in the many ways we may know it,
is to find fullness in the life that does.

The Bold

The bold are always loved,
even when they are hated.

The Free

It is only in truth that we can see what *is*.

It is only in truth that we can thrive as villains
in the false narratives others deem *should be*.

It is only in truth that we know peace.

This is freedom.

The Simple

Life is far simpler than we allow it to be. There is only truth and non-truth. That is all.

The Simple II

The greatest form of simplicity is found in living a
simple life without thinking with a simple mind.

The Passionate

Passion is a willingness to suffer for a purpose *beyond self.* It is not an excuse to act in shamelessness *for self.*

The Fatherly

The boy will serve his self
in recognition of his image.

The man will serve his kin
in recognition of his tribe.

The father will serve all
in no recognition at all.

The Redeemed

Underneath malevolence lays a greater evil,
boredom.

It is boredom that tempts the full into emptiness.

It is boredom that seduces the calm into restlessness.

It is boredom that breeds a meaninglessness so deep
that life, itself, is seen without its glory.

It is boredom, in its existential void of purpose,
that, once killed, gives life to redemption.

The Forgiving

To let go of yesterday
is to know forgiveness,
today.

To invite initiation into tomorrow
is to reconcile yesterday,
today.

To say goodbye to yesterday
is to release its control on our hearts,
today.

I must embrace this,
today.

The Wise

Sensationalism is our attempt drown out
meaninglessness with the noise of our own hysteria. It
clutters and darkens an otherwise clear sky.

The focused choose not to speak it.

The devoted choose not to see it.

The wise choose not to know it.

The Wise II

Perhaps wisdom is not just…

…the ability to acknowledge
the balance of opposing ideas
with an appetite to maintain it

…but the ability to understand
the nuance of absolute truth
without an appetite to abuse it.

The Symbolic

Observe not just the efforts of men,
but what such efforts reveal.

For all is a symbol,
reflective of a hierarchy of values,
and a message for eyes willing to see it.

The Loving

Hate is not always sour but always ill.

Love is not always sweet but always pure.

The hateful will *self* onto the other
as a projection of self, even if with a smile.

The loving will the good of the other
as the other, even if with a stern face.

The Strong

Strength is not only the ability to carry our own burdens, but to also carry the burdens of those who cannot carry their own.

The Certain

To act in accordance with nature is to fear the
uncertainty of the unknown.

To act in accordance with faith is to conquer such fear
with certainty beyond the unknown.

The Humble

Humility is not an act of nobility
but an embodiment of grace.

The Humble II

To recognize self, in the flaws of others,
is to acknowledge the absence of
divine favor of one over any other.

This is humility.

The Humble III

We seek favor above others, but I ask...

What is God's grace without the weight
of His righteous judgment?

What is God's love without the prospect
of His justified wrath?

The Powerful

In surrendering our thirst for power,
it is power we find.

The Virtuous

Virtue is not a public posture of nobility
entertained by cheap praise.

It is a private discipline anchored by its own
conviction.

The Truthful

Truth in conflict is still truth. Deception in agreement is still deception.

The recognition of truth is a choice. The consequence of deception is an inevitability.

The Truthful II

In an age concerned with value,
embrace meaning.

In an age occupied with facts,
seek truth.

The Graceful

Seeking to reason with the unreasonable is,
in it of itself, an unreasonable act.

To show grace to an unreasonable vessel is
to allow it to search for its way out of a house
locked from the inside…

…while welcoming the consequences that come with
declining its invitation into that house.

The Graceful II

Serving those, who will always return our favor,
is kindness.

Serving those, who will never return our favor,
is generosity.

Serving those, who will never know,
is grace.

The Graceful III

Those who receive grace seldom know it. For if they do, it is not grace but charity.

Those who give grace seldom speak of it. For if they do, it is not grace but vanity.

Grace often works in silence.

The Rested

Find rest not only in embracing the inevitabilities of tomorrow, but in letting go of hardships and the vanities of the past.

Simply, let go.

The Great

The greatest of decisions we make in this life
must not be those we're prepared to live with,
but those prepared to die with.

The Triumphant

Redemption is not a story of vengeance
but of triumph.

The Peaceful

One day, should we choose, we will see the world thru
the eyes of a child once again.

One day, should we choose, we will rediscover the
ability to laugh at our own lunacy.

One day, should we choose, we will embrace the
pleasures and the pains of this world *as it is.*

On this day, we will know,
we are living with peace.

On this day, we will know,
we are *living well.*

This is deliverance.

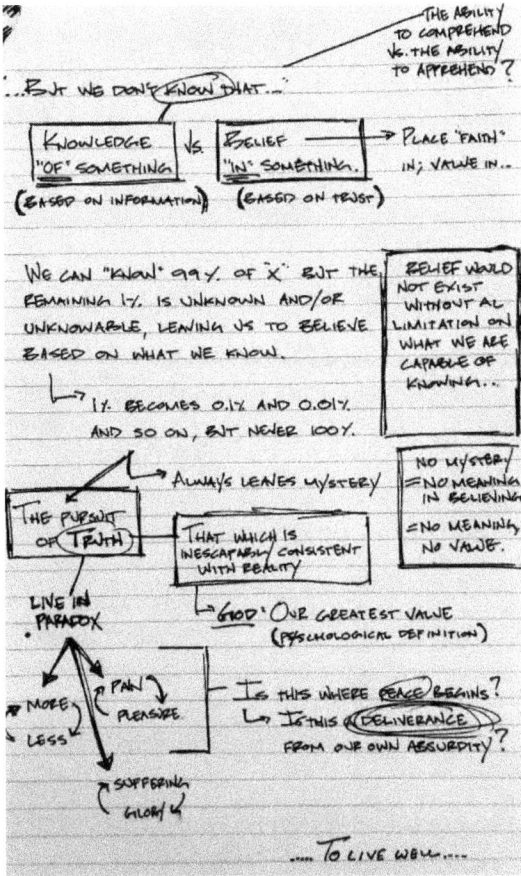

Seasons of Deliverance

...sometimes it's only a short story that must be told
for us to better understand this life...

DISCERNMENT

Two Knights

Two knights will always appear
at every crossed path.

...both riding white horses,
claiming to be a *Knight of Truth,*
and decrying the other
as a *Knight of Deception.*

...both offering the gift of a sword
and asking for the other to be slayed.

One will offer pain, alone,
and the other, pleasure, alone.

One will lead to heaven
and the other, to hell.

One will be chosen
and the other, killed.

This is discernment.

…sometimes it's only a few short flashes, within a foggy dream, that bring years of thought into frame…

A DREAM UNFORGOTTEN

A Blessing

In this dream, I heard your voice,
reminding me you said goodbye a long time ago.

I stood as a man but feared as a boy,
sprinting on a sinking iceberg.

You helped me to see,
no one is coming…

The winds blew while the night fell,
and hope began to fade.

The iceberg sank while the water rose,
and death placed its hand on my shoulder.

You helped me to see,
no one is coming…

I learned to swim in faith, not to drown in worry…
to carry others' pain, not to create my own…
to forgive, not to resent…

You helped me to see,
no one is coming…

I am forever grateful
for the blessing you gave me.

AN ECHO

"One day, when I was a young boy, I asked a man what I needed to learn, about life, so that I may grow up to *live well*. That man sat me down and said *'Son, living well is simply a matter of getting through the bullshit quicker.'*

I remember listening to those words as though they held the most profound insight I had ever heard. I remember thinking to myself, if I could only understand the layers of bullshit this man claimed to see, I could then understand life enough to *live well*.

Perhaps this collection of interpretations is an echo of that day…"

-Corey

GRATITUDE

Thank you for taking the time to read *Discernment: Seasons of Delusion, Devotion, and Deliverance*. Considering the fast-paced world we live in, constantly inundated with endless emails, calls, and notifications, I do not take for granted the time you took to read this short collection of interpretations.

If just one piece delivered the slighted of impact to the fashion in which you're interpreting life, others, or yourself, it would mean the world to me if you wouldn't mind recommending this book to a friend.

In truth,
Corey

ABOUT THE AUTHOR

Dr. Corey Castillo is a husband, a father, a business leader, a consultant, and an executive coach. As a consultant, he regularly partners with companies, of all industries, in enhancing overall organizational performance for scalable and sustainable results. As an executive coach, Corey partners with entrepreneurs, artists, business owners, and executive leaders in achieving their personal and professional goals. To know more, visit coreymcastillo.com.